Brian Moses lives in Sussex with his wife and two daughters. He claims that on one dark January night he was almost beamed up into an alien spaceship from a lay-by in the Ashdown Forest!

Lucy Maddison lives in Balham, London, with Brian the boyfriend, Patrick the lodger and Bubbles the cat.

ALIENS STOLE MY UNDERPANTS

AND OTHER INTERGALACTIC POEMS

chosen by Brian Moses

Illustrated by Lucy Maddison

MACMILLAN CHILDREN'S BOOKS

For Susie, Gaby and Lesley –
an intergalactic trio!

First published 1998
by Macmillan Children's Books
a division of Macmillan Publishers Ltd
25 Eccleston Place, London SW1W 9NF
and Basingstoke

Associated companies throughout the world

ISBN 0 330 34995 3

A CIP catalogue record for this book is available from the British Library.

Printed by Mackays of Chatham plc, Chatham, Kent.

'On Some Other Planet' and 'Rockets and Quasars' by John Rice
were first published in *Rockets and Quasars* by Aten Press 1984.

'The Blob' by Wes Magee was first published in *The Witch's Brew and other poems*
by Cambridge University Press 1989.

CONTENTS

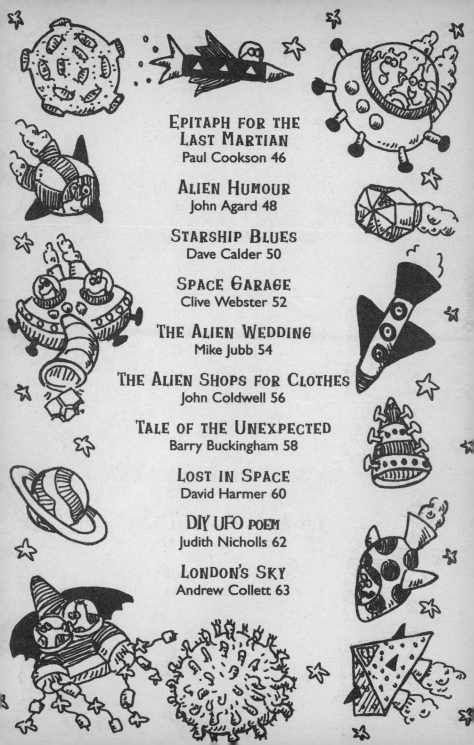

Rockets and Quasars

Rockets and quasars,
planets and stars,
I'm fed up with Earth
. . . so I'll see you on Mars!!

John Rice

New Kid at School

Last term we got a new kid at school.
Turned out to be a boy but we weren't sure at first.
It's difficult to tell when all the family have
green spotty skin, moustaches and eyes on stalks.

His name was 2£Bzz6gnnfqurjh.
Trouble was, no one could pronounce it properly,
even he couldn't, so he got nicknamed Clunk instead.

Clunk soon became popular in our class.
For one thing he was good at maths
and used to help us with our homework.
'Right, what's 4000 x 3.619 + 28.5 ÷ by the square root
   of 729?'
He'd press his nostril (the third on the left),
there'd be a bleep in his shirt
and a piece of paper would come out of his neck that
   said '537.2037037'.

He was so powerful he could even make school dinners
taste really nice with a click of his fingers
– all twenty-six of them.
Sparks would fly and with a zoom and a ping
cabbage would turn into ice cream
and sausages into chocolate bars.

Clunk was the sports day champion.
He broke the record for the 100m . . . 2.4 seconds,
won the three-legged race by himself
and then subdivided himself to the power of four
to win the relay
before sending the javelin, shot, discus and sandpit
into orbit with just one throw.
(It was on the news later that these items had been
photographed as UFOs and then hit twelve planes, three
helicopters and a hang-glider from Worksop.)

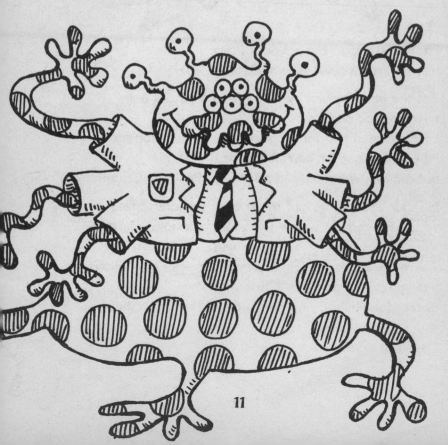

He was great on the school photo,
had his arms round all our class.

But the best day was when Hulk the school bully
tried to pick on him.
Clunk turned him into a poodle with pink ribbons.
Hulk didn't bother him after that,
but did follow him round asking for Pedigree Chum.

He didn't stay long, had to go back to outer space
where his dad got a new job as a black hole salesman.
We cried as we said our goodbyes.
There were tears in Clunk's eyes too – all nine of them.
We still get cards every Christmas,
except for Hulk . . . he gets a tin of Pedigree Chum.

Paul Cookson

THE YAFFLING YAHOO

A do-it-yourself space-rhyme

The Yaffling Yahoo
is a silly blue moo
but when she feels mean
she turns a bright . . . . . .

She shrinks herself small
when dry rain starts to fall.
She's an ugly disgrace
with those splumps on her . . . . . .

She enjoys a long drink
from a tank of pink ink,
then will sprint down the street
on her twelve pairs of . . . . . .

When her back gets an itch
then her nose starts to twitch.
She is skyscraper tall
yet as round as a . . . . . .

The Yaffling Yahoo
just hasn't a clue.
She continues to chase
through the dark depths of . . . . . .

Wes Magee

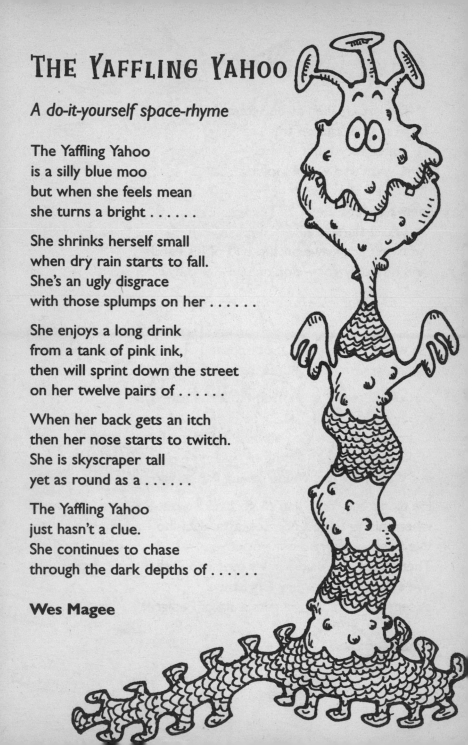

ALIEN EXCHANGE

We've got an alien at our school
he's on an exchange trip
I'd quite fancy him
if he wasn't so weird looking.
Just one head
only two legs
and no feelers at all
he hasn't got claws on the end of his hands
and he's only got – don't laugh - two eyes.

Can you believe that?
When we first saw him we fell about
but as our teacher says
we must be thoughtful and respect all visitors
to our galaxy
even if they have got only one feeding system
a breathing tube that is much too small
and horrid furry stuff on their head.

Next month my sister and I
are visiting his planet on the exchange.
It's got a funny name, Earth.
We've got to stay two weeks
our teacher says we must be careful
not to tread on the Earthlings by mistake
and always, always be polite
to raise our wings in greeting
and to put rubber tips on our sharpest horns.
I'm not looking forward to it much
the food looks awful
and the sea's dirty, not to mention the air.
Still, it'll make a change from boring old school
and perhaps some alien
will quite fancy me!

David Harmer

THE ALIEN TEACHER

Each night, Mr Potiphar peeled off his face
and commuted by rocket to outermost space.
Returning each morning, he screwed back his eyes
and reduced his antennae to minimum size.
Inserting his lungs, he would deeply inhale
while removing his gill flaps and shedding his tail.
After casting his skin with a writhe and a jerk,
he would dress himself smartly and drive off to work.
He worked as a teacher. The Head was no fool.
She employed only aliens to teach at her school.
'They are better than Earthlings,' I heard her remark.
'They have far larger brains and can see in the dark
and the pupils get day trips to Luna or Mars
and sightseeing jaunts to the furthermost stars.
They're developing talents like reading the mind,
teleportation and things of that kind,
and (the Head quivered with ill-restrained mirth)
we plan in due course, to take over the Earth.'

Marian Swinger

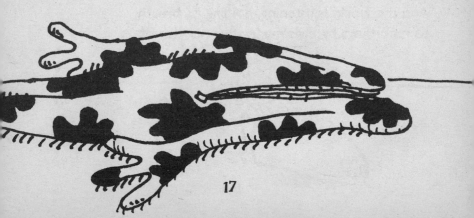

ELVIS IS BACK!

Rumours persist in the press that the rock singer Elvis Presley faked his death. One of the most bizarre ideas is that Elvis was in touch with aliens and that they came down to Earth to spirit him away! One day, of course, he may decide to stage a comeback!

When aliens brought Elvis Presley back
it looked as if we were under attack
as a mother ship of incredible size
sank down to Earth right in front of our eyes,
and it really gave us an almighty shock
when out of its doors stepped the King of Rock.

There was laughter, tears and celebration,
Elvis is back, he's been on vacation.
There he stood looking leaner and fitter,
Elvis is back, in a suit made of glitter.
It seems the doubters were right all along,
Elvis is back with a dozen new songs.

He's been cutting an album somewhere in space,
now he's bringing it home to the human race.
And the world is listening, holding its breath,
to recordings by Elvis made after his 'death'.

And of course he'd duped us all into thinking
it was pills and burgers and too much drinking
that killed him off, but that wasn't the case,
Elvis escaped to a different place.
He's been touring out there, a star upon stars,
rocking the universe, Venus to Mars.

And as alien ships descend from above
we're sending out our message of love
and hoping they'll show no desire to attack,
but we don't really care because ELVIS IS BACK!

Brian Moses

DEAR ALIEN

I newly learn your Earth-Speak —
forgive if I get it wrong.
When I don't know the Earth-word
I shall have to write in *Sprong*.

Sorry to start 'Dear Alien',
but now our planets are twinned,
I hope as we get to know each other
we shall want to write 'Dear *fribble*'.

I am thirty-two, in *Sprong*-years;
in Earth-years, I'd be eight.
My mum's one-hundred-and-twenty today
so we're going to celebrate.

She's invited us all to a *poggle*,
and baked a birthday cake,
with a hundred and twenty *clabbits* on top.
(Is my Earth-speak without a mistake?)

Me, please, to tell what I wrong get,
my lovely new pen-*fribble*.
I want to learn all about Earth.
Write and tell me all your *gribble*.

I shall now tell you what I look like:
my hair is short and red
on my arms and legs, and greenish-*grump*
and curly on my head.

My ecklings are blue and yellow,
with the middle one black and white.
I'm told that Earthlings have only two —
can you really see all right?

I have a brother and sister,
and a lovely pet *splink* called Bloggs.
Is it true you have pets with four legs and a tail?
What do you call them — *droggs*?

Please write back soon, dear Earthling,
don't keep me waiting long —
and remember to tell me your Earth-words
that, today, I've written in *Sprong*.

Celia Warren

sprong

THE BLOB

And . . . what is it like?

  Oh, it's scary and fatbumped
  and spike-eared and groany.
  It's hairy and face-splumped
  and bolshy and bony.

And . . . where does it live?

  Oh, in comets and spaceships
  and pulsars and black holes.
  In craters and sheepdips
  and caverns and north poles.

And . . . what does it eat?

  Oh, roast rocks and fishlegs
  and X-rays and mooncrust.
  Then steelmeat and sun-eggs
  and lava and spacedust.

And . . . who are its enemies?

Oh, Zonkers and Moonquakes
and Sunquarks and Zigbags.
Dumb Duncers and Milkshakes
and Smogsters and Wigwags.

And . . . and . . . what does it wear?

Not a thing!
It's bare!

Wes Magee

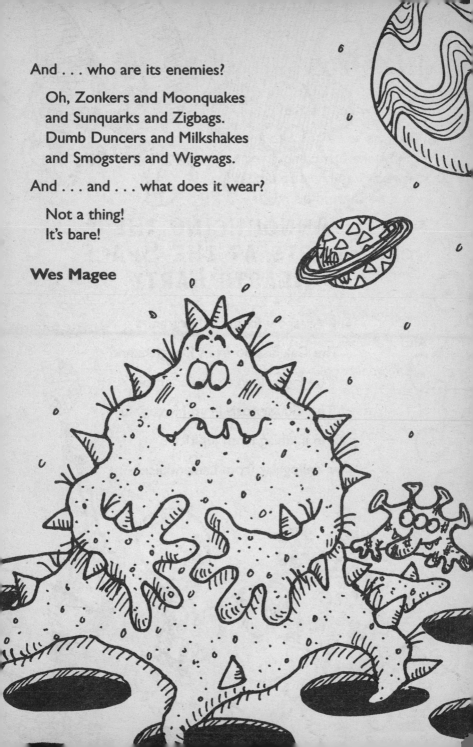

ANNOUNCING THE GUESTS AT THE SPACE BEASTS' PARTY

'The Araspew from Bashergrannd'

'The Cakkaspoo from Danglebannd'

'The Eggisplosh from Ferrintole'

'The Gurglenosh from Hiccupole'

'The Inkiblag from Jupitickle'

'The Kellogclag from Lamandpickle'

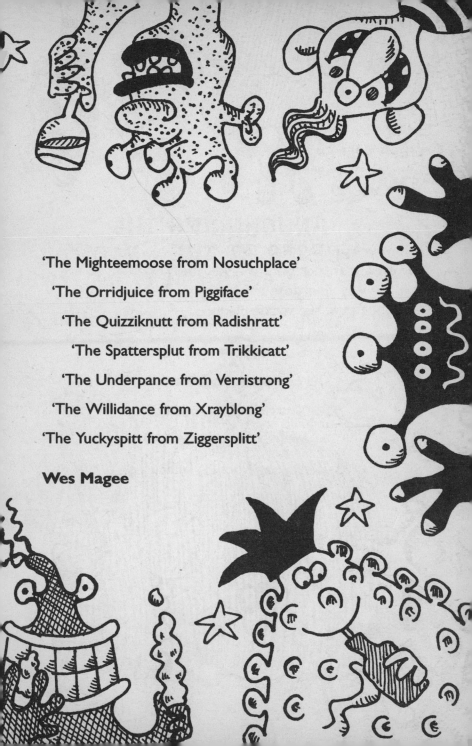

'The Mighteemoose from Nosuchplace'

'The Orridjuice from Piggiface'

'The Quizziknutt from Radishratt'

'The Spattersplut from Trikkicatt'

'The Underpance from Verristrong'

'The Willidance from Xrayblong'

'The Yuckyspitt from Ziggersplitt'

Wes Magee

ALIEN LOVE POEMS

I

Ribblerabbles are red
Vorglesmoogs are blue
Borglemilk is sweet
And so are you

2

I love your lips like yellow jelly
Your eyes, that stick out from your belly
I love the way your nose inflates
I love your ears, like vuckle plates

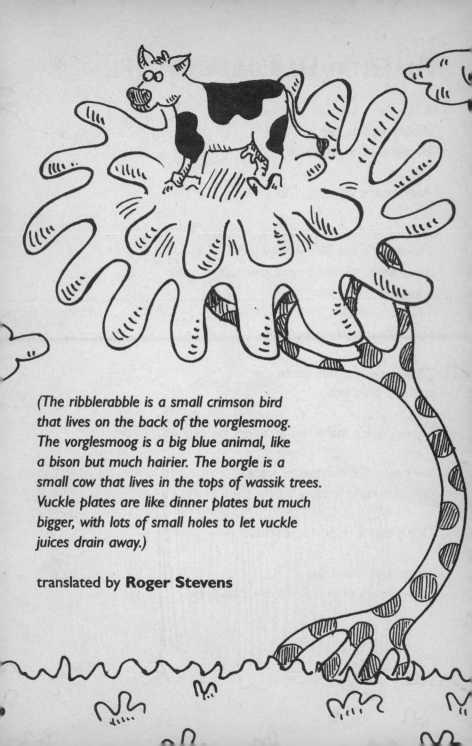

(The ribblerabble is a small crimson bird
that lives on the back of the vorglesmoog.
The vorglesmoog is a big blue animal, like
a bison but much hairier. The borgle is a
small cow that lives in the tops of wassik trees.
Vuckle plates are like dinner plates but much
bigger, with lots of small holes to let vuckle
juices drain away.)

translated by **Roger Stevens**

MY STEP-DAD IS AN ALIEN

I'd suspected for some time.
I finally got up the courage
to talk to him about it.

I think you're an alien, I told him.

Nonsense, he said. Why do you think that?

*You're bald. You don't have any hair
anywhere.*

That's not unusual, he said.

*Well, you've got one green eye
and one blue one.*

That doesn't make me an alien, he replied.

*You can make the toaster work
without turning it on.*

That's just a trick, he smiled.

*Sometimes I hear you
talking to Mum in a weird alien language.*

I'm learning Greek
and Mum lets me practise on her.

What about your bright blue tail?

Ah, he said thoughtfully.
You're right, of course.
So, the tail gave it away, did it?

Roger Stevens

DO I LOOK
LIKE AN
ALIEN!

ALIENS STOLE MY UNDERPANTS

To understand the ways
of alien beings is hard,
and I've never worked it out
why they landed in my backyard.

And I've always wondered why
on their journey from the stars,
these aliens stole my underpants
and took them back to Mars.

They came on a Monday night
when the weekend wash had been done,
pegged out on the line
to be dried by the morning sun.

Mrs Driver from next door
was a witness at the scene
when aliens snatched my underpants –
I'm glad that they were clean!

It seems they were quite choosy
as nothing else was taken.
Do aliens wear underpants
or were they just mistaken?

I think I have a theory
as to what they wanted them for,
they needed to block off a draught
blowing in through the spacecraft door.

Or maybe some Mars museum
wanted items brought back from space.
Just think, my pair of Y-fronts
displayed in their own glass case.

And on the label beneath
would be written where they got 'em
and how such funny underwear
once covered an Earthling's bottom!

Brian Moses

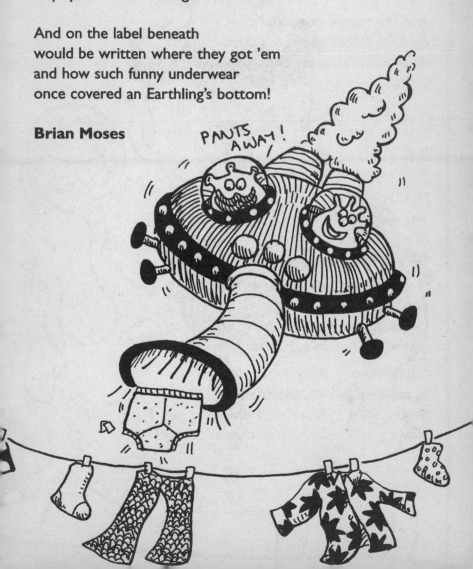

vALIENtine

An alien valentine in verse
from elsewhere in the universe.
(Heavens above. It must be love.)

Dear Alien, I love you
with your 13 legs
and your hair so blue
and your beautiful tentacles
covered with goo.

In all of inner or outer space
there cannot be so fair a face
with ears stuck on all over the place.

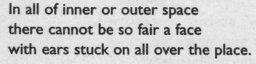

So let me be your satellite
revolving round you every night.
Tell me yes. Ah, tell me soon.
For you, my dear, I'm over the moon.

Thinking of you, I cannot sleep.
Yours X-static-ly,

E.T. BLEEP

Tony Mitton

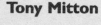

THE ANSWER IS

ABDUCTED BY ALIENS

When Jack came back to school
after one day's absence, unexplained,
he went and told his teacher
he'd been abducted by aliens.
She told him not to be so daft,
but he gave us all the details –
what the spacecraft had looked like,
how extra-terrestrials kidnapped him
then carried him onto their ship.
And Jack told his story
again and again. 'When they landed,' he said,
'I was terrified, couldn't move,
I nearly died, then a blade of light
cut the night in two, trapped me
in its beam so I couldn't see. I felt
arms that were rubbery wrapped around me,
like the coils of our garden hose.

And I don't recall anything more
till I found myself back on the ground
while rasping voices were telling me
that everything I saw they would see,
that everything I heard they would hear,
that everything I ate they would taste.
And I know they're out there watching me,
in some intergalactic laboratory.
I'm a subject for investigation
constantly sending back information,
a bleep that bleeps on a bank of screens,
abducted by aliens, tagged and then freed.'

'What nonsense you talk,' his teacher said.
'Take out your books, who's ready for maths?'
But Jack couldn't make his figures come right.
If communication works both ways, he thought,
then he might benefit too —
maybe aliens could help solve his multiplication!

Brian Moses

On Some Other Planet

On some other planet
near some other star,
there's a music-loving alien
who drives a blue car.

On some other planet
on some far distant world,
ther's a bright sunny garden
where a cat lies curled.

On some other planet
a trillion miles away,
there are parks and beaches
where the young aliens play.

On some other planet
in another time-zone,
there are intelligent beings
who feel very much alone.

On some other planet
one that we can't see,
there must be one person
who's a duplicate of me.

John Rice

37

STARWALKER

My cat's an extra-terrestrial.
He walks the stars at night.
He plants one paw on Betelgeuse
for it is his by right.

Swishing his tail, he dusts the moon
and sweeps the clouds away.
A second paw covers Jupiter.
'It's mine,' he seems to say.

He polishes the evening stars,
so they can light the earth.
His third paw toys with Mercury,
the planet of his birth.

His nightly prowl complete at last,
he gives a mighty sneeze,
and with his fourth paw scratches
his extra-terrestrial fleas.

Janis Priestley

THE SPACESHIP WITH L-PLATES

A spaceship with L-plates came juddering down
and flattened a cornfield a few miles from town.
Out stepped an alien, Zozzimus Glop,
who had grievously botched his emergency stop.
'An Earthling could fly this crate better than you,'
his examiner bellowed, her head turning blue.
As she shouted, she noticed (congealing with fear)
a quivering figure. 'Hoy! Come over here.'
And the figure (a schoolgirl called Madeline Pike)
came tottering over, still pushing its bike.
'Inside,' the examiner barked. 'Come this way.
I'll train you to fly by the end of the day.'
The ship shimmered skywards without any sound
leaving just Zozzimus Glop on the ground.
It returned in the evening, alighting with ease
near where Zozzimus Glop perched, concealed,
  in the trees.

The examiner shouted, 'Glop. Come here you fool.
This Earthling, as soon as she's finished with school,
will be training with us on our starship in space.'
Zozzimus slouched to the ship in disgrace.
But future commander, proud Madeline Pike,
gave a salute and went home on her bike.

Marian Swinger

THE ALIEN FOOTBALL TEAM

I'm in the alien football team.
All of us have five feet.
We run at a hundred miles an hour.
We're the team no one can beat.

We don't need to shout to get the ball –
we're telepathic instead.
We've got X-ray vision to see through defenders
and eyes in the back of our head.

We haven't ever bought a transfer
and I'm sure we never will.
How could you ever improve a team
that usually wins ninety–nil!

We've won the double double double
dozens of years on the run.
The trouble is that winning so easily
really isn't much fun.

You'd think an unbroken record like ours
was the ideal one to choose,
but we get so bored. How nice it would be,
just even once, to lose.

Charles Thomson

OUT OF A CLOUD

I have never seen one,
Desmond saw one though,
He said it hummed like hives of bees,
He said it glowed a glow,
He said it swooped out of a cloud
And lit the fields below,
He said it took his heart away,
Desmond's UFO.

Of course no one believed him,
But wandering here and there,
Desmond scanned the sky each night
With his hopeful stare,
Examining the Milky Way,
Venus, the Plough, the Bear,
Searching, wishing, longing,
Desmond head-in-air.

And then, one day, he vanished.
How? We'll never know.
We found no clue or trace of him,
Hunting high and low,
Except, spiked on a barbed-wire fence,
A note saying: 'Told you so,'
And all around the grass pressed down . . .
Where did Desmond go?

Richard Edwards

EPITAPH FOR THE LAST MARTIAN

Crash landing caused extinction
The last of the Martian species
Here and here and here and here
He rests in pieces.

Paul Cookson

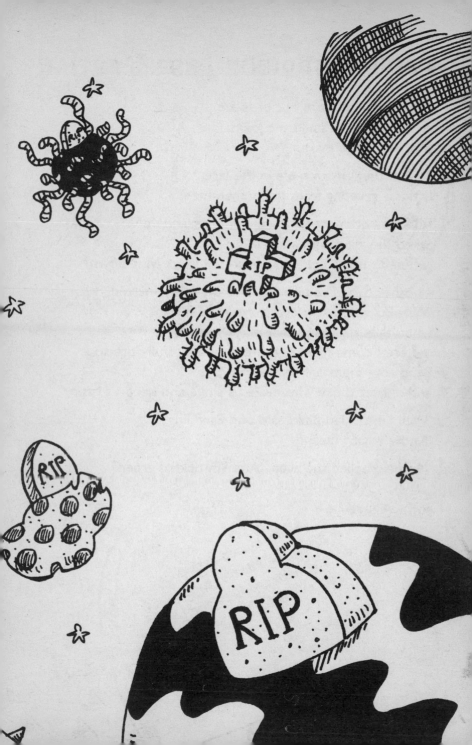

Alien Humour

A visiting alien from out of space
could not understand the jokes
that Earthlings make.

'When they throw a pie in the face,
is this a greeting from the human race?

And why do most Earthling comics stand up,'
asked the alien with a frown,
'when it's more comfortable to tell jokes lying down?

Another thing I've noticed,' said the alien amazed.
'Why do you throw eggs at your politicians
when they say things that make you angry?
Where I come from eggs are so wonderfully precious
we throw them only on festive days
and only at those who make us smile and keep us happy.'

'Well I'm tickled pink,' said one Earthling.
'Know what I mean?'

'Maybe,' replied the alien. 'And I'm tickled green.'

John Agard

STARSHIP BLUES

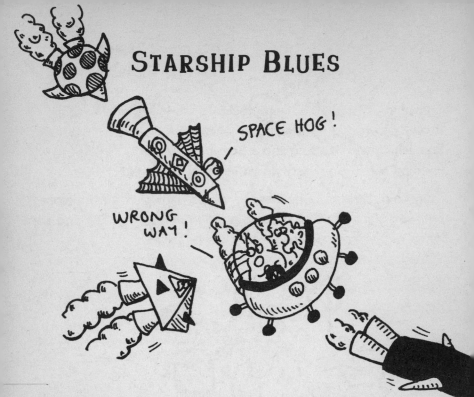

It's hard out on a spaceship, couldn't get much worse,
All we get to see is the same old universe.

The food tastes like rubber and looks like concrete tiles
We only change our spacesuits every million million miles
The captain's going crazy, he thinks we're crocodiles
The doctor's seeing double, the atomic drive's got piles.

We've been light years in a rocket-jam on the Milky Way
It's 'Watch that star!' and 'Mind that sun!' all day
We never get back home, we never see our pay
The ones we left behind have all turned old and grey.

Our ship's computer's happy, it thinks it's made of cheese
It only answers questions put in ancient Japanese
Something with no face and a horrible disease
is doing something nasty down in the deep-freeze.

They told us we'd be heroes, go where none had gone before
but we sit and stare at starscreens till our eyes are red and sore
Sirius or Saturn, I don't care any more,
if it wasn't for the black holes life would be a bore.

There's a jelly in my cabin, it's eaten up my berth
Beam me up, beam me down, beam me back to earth.

Dave Calder

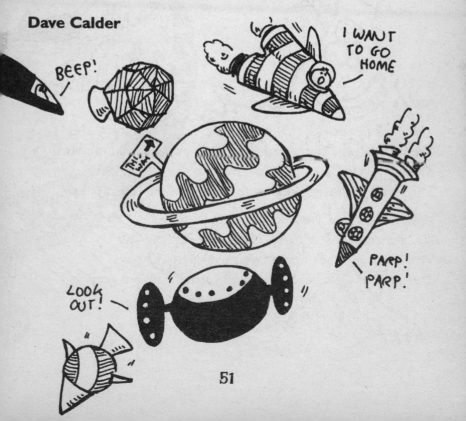

Space Garage

The garage for second-hand spaceships
Was trying to sell off its stock.
They advertised, 'One careful owner,
Only one billion miles on the clock ...'

Clive Webster

FOR SALE

THE ALIEN WEDDING

When the aliens got married,
The bride was dressed in zeet;
And with a flumzel in her groyt,
She really looked a treat.

The groom was onggy spoodle,
He felt a little quenz;
The best man told him not to cronk
In front of all their friends.

The bride's ensloshid father
Had slupped down too much glorter;
He grobbled up the aisle alone,
Then flomped back for his daughter.

The lushen bridesmaids followed
With such wigantic walks;
Their optikacious oggers
Were sparkling on their stalks.

The bride and groom entroathed their splice,
They swapped a little squip;
Then he splodged her on the kisser,
And she flimped him on the blip.

And after the wedding breakfast,
The stroadling and the laughter,
The loving pair took off to Mars,
And splayed winkerly ever after.

Mike Jubb

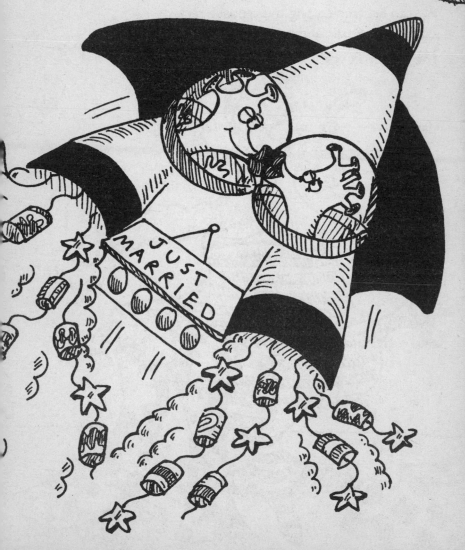

THE ALIEN SHOPS FOR CLOTHES

The alien raised a tentacle and opened the door
Of a famous London fashion store
He glanced at the jackets on the smart suit rail,
Checked out the sweaters in the half-price sale.
He ran his trunk along the trouser rack
Picked out a pair and put them back.
He flicked through the socks with his one blue claw,

He sniffed the T-shirts and began to roar,
'I wanted something casual, off the peg.
Denim or cotton with just the one leg.'
The alien rolled his three red eyes.
'But you don't stock anything in my size.
And another thing, before I leave
Your sweaters all need an extra sleeve.
The Spring Collection is a total disgrace,
It only caters for the human race!'
He oozed from the store and hailed a taxi
And did the rest of his shopping in another galaxy.

John Coldwell

MAYBE SIR
SHOULD TRY
A LARGER
SIZE?

TALE OF THE UNEXPECTED

The Martians are a-coming —
they're running down the street.
Their blasters are a-gleaming,
and there's red dust on their feet.

Terrestrials scitter-scatter,
for there's panic all about.
Pink Martian eyes are goggling;
purple tongues flick in and out.

What brings these aliens Earthwards?
No, it isn't what you think.
They've just popped down for fish and chips,
and a can of fizzy drink.

Barry Buckingham

LOST IN SPACE

When the spaceship first landed
nose down in Dad's prize vegetables
I wasn't expecting the pilot
to be a large blue blob with seven heads
the size and shape of rugby balls
and a toothy grin on his fourteen mouths.

'Is this Space Base Six?' he asked.
'No,' I said, 'it's our back garden, number fifty-two.'
'Oh,' he said, 'are you sure?'
and took from his silver overalls
a shiny book of maps.

There were routes round all the galaxies
ways to the stars through deepest space
maps to planets I'd never heard of
maps to comets, maps to moons
and short cuts to the sun.

'Of course,' he said, 'silly me,
I turned right, not left, at Venus,
easily done, goodbye.'
He shook his heads, climbed inside,
the spaceship roared into the sky
and in a shower of leeks and cabbages
disappeared for ever.

David Harmer

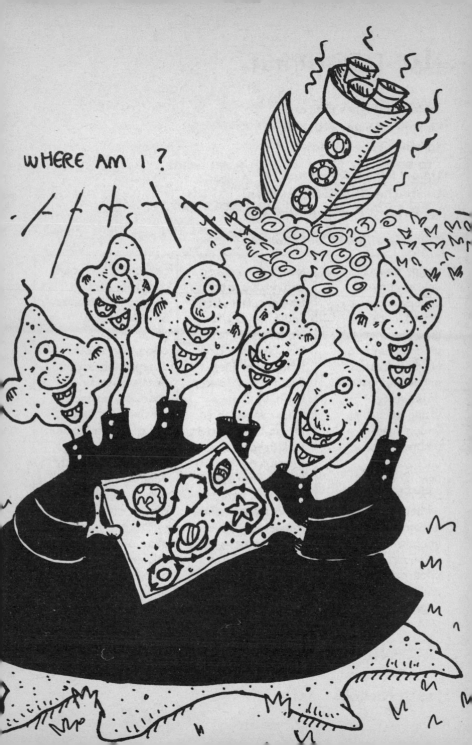

DIY UFO Poem

Umbrella Fights Officer?
Unapproachable Fish Offside?
Uncanny Frog Objects?

Unfold Furled Omelette?
Unattached Fabulous Oarsman?
Underpants Fumigate Oldham?

Try your own DIY UFO Poem!

upside down, unlikely, unload, underground, united, uncle, uncanny, uncertain, ultimate, unbolt, Hugh, unbeaten, unbutton, unaware, unassuming, unapproachable, under, unable, umbrella, under, unattached, ugly, ultimate, unwind, unscramble, unmentionable, unconscious, uncork, unlikely, underground, underpants, undeveloped, understand, unfold, unique . . .	fade, fish, fashionable, fabric, fabulous, face, facts, fiddle, fail, fair/fare, fat, fall, false, fame, feel, faint, ferocious, fit, fill, film, fine, find, fix, first, flatten, flood, fly, fume, follow, foggy, force, forget, forge, forfeit, foul, fighting, free, fritter, frog, fry, fuse, funnel, futuristic, fuzzy, fun, fumigate, frolic, front, friendly, frequently, frizzle, first, flibberty-gibbet, formidable, form, forlorn, foreign, first, French, foreboding, foolish, fraudulent . . .	obligation, oak, oath, oarsman, oar, oatmeal, obedient, obelisk, obesity, observation, oboe, obnoxious, obscure, observant, ocean, obsession, obsolete, obstacle, obstinacy, obvious, occasion, occupation, office, occupant, October, octuplets, odd, oddball, ode, other, offence, offer, official, offside, offshore, offspring, okay, okapi, oil, Oldham, Olympic, omelette, one-stop, ozone, opposite, onomatopoeia, ooze, outrageous . . .
UNIDENTIFIED	FLYING	OBJECT

Judith Nicholls

LONDON'S SKY

A UFO came speeding
in the dead of night,
turned left at the pillar-box
then first right.

Shooting down the high street
lighting London's sky,
a giant, marshmallow shape;
one overgrown pork pie.

And slowing down a little,
as out jumped tiny men,
green and yellow, just one eye,
all heading for Big Ben.

Sliding down its towers,
across its moonlit face
to set their watches one more time
before shooting back to space.

Andrew Collett

A selected list of poetry books available from Macmillan

The prices shown below are correct at the time of going to press. However, Macmillan Publishers reserve the right to show new retail prices on covers which may differ from those previously advertised.

The Secret Lives of Teachers
Revealing rhymes, chosen by Brian Moses £3.50

'Ere we Go!
Football poems, chosen by David Orme £2.99

You'll Never Walk Alone
More football poems, chosen by David Orme £2.99

Nothing Tastes Quite Like a Gerbil
And other vile verses, chosen by David Orme £2.99

Custard Pie
Poems that are jokes, chosen by Pie Corbett £2.99

Tongue Twisters and Tonsil Twizzlers
Poems chosen by Paul Cookson £2.99

All Macmillan titles can be ordered at your local bookshop or are available by post from:

Book Service by Post
PO Box 29, Douglas, Isle of Man IM99 1BQ

Credit cards accepted. For details:
Telephone: 01624 675137
Fax: 01624 670923
E-mail: bookshop@enterprise.net

Free postage and packing in the UK.
Overseas customers: add £1 per book (paperback)
and £3 per book (hardback).